T0368364

MESSIAH

Patrick Marks

authorHOUSE

AuthorHouse™ UK
1663 Liberty Drive
Bloomington, IN 47403 USA
www.authorhouse.co.uk
Phone: UK TFN: 0800 0148641 (Toll Free inside the UK)
  UK Local: (02) 0369 56322 (+44 20 3695 6322 from outside the UK)

Published by AuthorHouse   04/24/2025

ISBN: 979-8-8230-8546-5 (sc)
ISBN: 979-8-8230-8547-2 (e)

Library of Congress Control Number: 2023921583

Print information available on the last page.

Contents

Contents

And tell me He they crucified
Was raised and lives today
It burns within my heart
To think I'll see Him some sweet day;
For HE gave His life And His words to me
Brought life into my soul
The days are so much brighter now
Since that day He made me whole.

Oh What A Saviour

They came from afar
By means of a star
The wise men had sought
Gifts they had brought
the one they awaited
To God be related
At last they would see
The one who would be their Saviour

Oh what a Saviour
God showed His favour
Sending His Son, Jesus

Oh how they worshipped
In fellowship so sweet
Angels transcended
Shepherds attended
Magi knee bended
Their journey's ended
In manger lay
The Life, Truth, The Way, JESUS

Oh what a Saviour
God showed His favour
Sending His Son, JESUS

And we remember
A day in December
A Son to us given
On earth God was livin'

1

He came to save us
And so he forgave us
To Bethlehem came
Who took the blame, Jesus.

Oh what a Saviour
God showed His favour
Sending His Son, Jesus.

Message foretold
In times of old
Prophet and priest
Magi from the east
A Saviour was promised
God ever honest
Glorious King
Oh how we'd sing, Jesus.

Qh what a Saviour
God showed His favour
Sending His Son, Jesus.

In Glory ending
Our mansion attending
His Father hand lending
Our sojourn ending
As magi from the East
Our journey will cease
Before his throne
He'll claim his own, Jesus.

Oh what a Saviour
God showed His favour
Sending His Son, Jesus.

Oh what a Saviour
God showed His favour
Sending His Son, Jesus.

Remembrance

It seems they have forgotten you
When the wreath is set in place
Oh don't they know, that you did go
To die for all our race
No chosen face or select place
You love us all the same
No favourite caste you died at last
To bring us home again.

Where are they now
The thankful ones
Remembering those
Who fought with guns
But your's The Sacrifice Supreme
And on Your head a crown does gleam
A Heavenly Home, a Royal Throne
But to those you died for
What does it mean.

Now is the time
The Hour Sublime
The scorn, the thorn, the tree
We will remember, Thee.

7

Ransomed / He took my place

I came to the counter
And saw you there
Tears in your eyes
A look of despair
I said to the man
"What price must I pay
For this hopeless boy
Who in life fell astray."
He said "A King's ransom
Will only release
Dry the boy's tears
And bring to him peace."
"Well I am the King
I will bear his disgrace
Let the boy go
And I will take his place."

Sit by my side
And I'll tell you a story
Of a Lamb that was slain
So that we might share His Glory.

Jesus came down
He was born in a manger
He dwelt among His own
But to His own a stranger.

To Calvary He came
That stranger became their Saviour
And now he sits in Glory
Leaving me to tell the Story.

Many years have passed
Since I was last
Upon the scene of time
But I've not changed
I'm still the same
Wishing you were mine.

Come and see
Look at me
The nail prints in my hands
I paid the price
The sacrifice
Oh can't you understand.

Only One Way
There was to pay
That we might bring you in
I had to come
To be THE One
To die for all your sin

And here I stand
In outstretched hand
A pardon full and free;
Come take the step
Eternal Life accept
Purchase of from Me.

Jesus, Author and Finisher of our FAITH
To Thee we come for mercy
And grace in time of need;
The enemy would assail us
Accuse us before your Throne
To our gracious Advocate
We dare would might our plead

Thou hast no voice but our voices
To sound the gospel call
Of a Father's call to wayward sons
Repentance one and all

I have no news but His views
The way is clear to all
Surrender now the good news accept
There is no other way

And to the Spirit I would lean
Whoever pleads for me
To help in my infirmities
And knows for what to pray;
I have the endless assurance
That my Saviour remonstrates for me

Sweet joy of all the ages
The theme of endless song
I readily cast my lot in
And to you safely belong
The enemy may accuse me
But Thou my advocate be
Who can dare oppose me
When you're my endless plea

Happy in the knowledge
You plead my every cause
I stand apart and wonder
And ever lead applause.

Oh thank you advocate, Master
The Shepherd of the fold
Who laid down your life
For a myriad souls untold

You have no arms but our arms
To carry the message forth
To tell of endless love
That secures our second birth

Oh, Jesus, may I be faithful
Throughout the coming days
And plead Thy might strengthen
To follow all your ways.

Oh Calvary's tree, what mercy see
And sins beyond recall
Thou dost erase of every phase
The iniquities of us all.

And thanks abound, l will be found
Before the throne of grace
To shed my crown, and prostrate down
Ere see my Saviour's face.

Honour, majesty, glory bring
And to the King our tributes sing;
Hail Him as our matchless Lord
And to Him serve in one accord.

He lifts me up when I'm brought low
He gives me strength, and where to go;
I can but trust in Him for grace
He calls me nigh to see HIS face

Jesus, Saviour, Master, King
And to your feet bring everything;
Our mortal souls you ransomed fair
Oh, just to see Your face up there

I scarce conceive, yet will believe
You vanquished death with your last breath;
What sacrifice, what awesome price
I gladly bow in homage now.

You are the sovereign who reigns on high,
To manger came, a stable sty;
Yet high above you rule the sky
Were I to trust, you'll never die.

A place prepared, l knew you cared
And soon to be a Heaven shared
I scarce imagine what it will be
But greater far Thy face to see.

I will but hail, joy unconfined
My sins are passed long put behind;
I only joy my Saviour see
And Heaven to spend in Eternity

Alas, the joy in Heaven to be
With friends, and famed around to see;
I will rejoice, my soul set free,
The bliss of Heaven is mine to be.

Jesus came into this life
And sought Himself, no, not a wife
He walked the streets and hills nearby
There was no place for Him to lie.

Loved He the world, no one could still
The zeal to do His Father's will;
And so He left Gethsemane
Went all the way to Calvary.

Thank you, Jesus for the cross
Thank you, Jesus for the loss
Of a life you freely gave
For a world you came to save.

Oh, wonder l, that you should die,
For such a one, oh unworthy l;
But oh, it' true, thank God it's true;
And Jesus, l'll be thanking you all Eternity through.

Christ Jesus I remember
The life you laid on earth
The peril and the purpose
The love that due it's course.

In reverie my eyes do see
The pain you had to bear
I scarce conceive I will believe
The love that hung you there.

My thanks abound, l will them sound
From year, to year, to year;
I can't but speak, l won't be meek
To remember you suffered there.

And brighter still, that day until
I see my Saviour's face
The pain he bore, imprints the more
Upon my grateful heart.

What love divine was your's and mine
At Calvary, upon the tree;
I scarce can see He died for me
And as for you, He saw it through.

What love divine, there's no so fine
I will it take this bread to break;
Oh, Master, please, impart with ease
The thorn I see partook for me.

What tears I shed as your blood red
Flows from the cross to pay for loss;
Oh love divine, of godly sign
Demands my all beyond recall.

What thanks I owe, what lengths to go
Heaven's host witness the most;
And of their praise, and Heaven raise
Salute the KING, His spoils to bring.

I wade into the wash of your words
And worry, and weariness wither away.
The gentle touch of truth transforms me
Till I am transfixed by the treasures therein.
It exceeds, exhorts earlier experience
Extends enriches as I exercise within.
Oh bless the bliss of brilliant light
That beams before my benefitting being
Thank you, Godly Father; Most High; Love;
Worthy Warrior; Brave Titan of Heaven and Eternity.

I breast stroke to part the waves
Of your worthy washing waters,
Enriched by the exercise
Of wading close to Thee
Till I transfixed;
No more need draw nearer;
Oh, behold your blessed beaming gaze
And know I'm Home.

How you must love us
To part with Him this way
Our ugly sin has ushered in
This heinous way to pay.

Everlasting thankfulness
Remembrance of His death
To follow and to praise Him
Until my final breath.

And when I rise to meet Him
Who did so much for me
We will embrace, to see His face
Is all Eternity for me.

Oh the news is just stupendous
And the multitude tremendous
Make haste to sound the call
Christ was crucified for all.

How in mercy to set free
Crucified for you and me
So that we could ever be
Clothed in love eternally.

Now the triumph we must raise
Of how Jesus can erase
The vilest sin to welcome in
Bestow his righteousness within.

All the saints will gather there
Those of old from everywhere;
Tell of mercy, free from sin
How the Father welcomes in.

In Thy salvation I glory and shall prevail
I cannot see the future, just what it shall entail;
But this I know, He who overcame shall be my guide;
And in His steps press on, as He is ever by my side.

Truly I rejoice, l see the end in sight
My Kingdom, my Redeemer awaits beyond the night;
Doom and gloom I banish, enemies of Hell
I shall prevail heavenward, still my Saviour's tale to tell.

I may not see the shore, but I press on before;
Nor see the hordes of Hell, but vanquish and do well.
Assail the might adversary, who pierced my King at Calvary;
Right to the jubilant end we valiantly contend
In sight our Hope, and we will cope
With Jesus to the end.

The One who calmed the sea, did die for me;
Who healed the paralyzed, and made the blind to see;
That came from above, of mercy, right, and Love;
It is God's only Son, and it's us He's thinking of.

I treasure every moment, but especially Calvary,
Where He scaled the heights to rescue sorry me.
Thank you, ever thank you, Great Lamb of Calvary;
To exalt and ever praise you, happy I will be,
To share the comforts of Heaven you've prepared for me
Come round, the door is open, ever open for Thee.

Today's the day I give my Son away
We planned it before, now there's no more, time to delay.

The universe groans, and all He owns, will restore alone
The day HE dies, darkens the skies, a new day to dawn.

Mercy was found, and He'll be crowned King of all Kings
Untold bliss, l would not miss, this glorious Day.

Now I can see, how He died for me on Calvary;
No other way, He had to pay for it all.

And some day soon, I will behold this Jesus,
The one who gave His sacred life for me'

I'll raise Him up, l'll praise Him up for all Eternity.

Jesus, you mean the world to me
My love, my life, I present
To be, and do whatever you wish
From now is my firm intent.

And so by your spirit as my guide
And grace to lead the way
To pursue the path of righteousness
And of your kingdom say

May every soul find your way
And safely journey home
Sufficient is your death to pay
And never again to roam.

And songs employ, heralding such joy
Our Saviour in Heaven again
A Glorious Day not far away
His face to see so plain.

They gathered there that Christmas morn
Shepherds and angels a stable adorn
A light in the heavens illumines the scene
What wondrous beginning, so much it would mean.

Humble estate for a tavern room too late
This circumstance God leaves nothing to chance
No privileged arrival, God's Son born in a stable
Message foretold, so the story would hold.

Virgin Mother Mary, her carpenter husband Joseph
A time to rejoice, a righteous couple God's choice;
No cosy inception, a heavenly reception
Singing god's praises a myriad angels raises.

How could I love you more
My countrymen, I you implore
Be ye reconciled to God
Before you return unto the sod.

God was in Christ
None can free from His fist
Accept the offer not to be missed
Hear this call, please don't resist.

What more, what more
The cross of Calvary sore
Oh God, at them everything I wield
To you Jesus everything I yield.

Such love, what dove, from above
What pain what strain, for our gain
So sore, what more, l you implore
Oh save, off stave, this I crave.

Oh Calvary, what mercy see, for eternity
For you, for you, for you;
In Jesus' name, who took our blame,
And bore our shame, eternal fame
Grasp it, clasp it, nor Satan asp it
Amen hallelujah.

And though at times I've failed Him
Yet He's been there all along
To render His forgiveness
He will ever be my song.

The Blessed man of Calvary
The Saviour of my soul
A friend who'll never leave me
And who came to make me whole.

Mercy, love, compassion
Flow from Him I see
A forgiving glance, another chance,
Sure He died to set me free.

And through unending Glory
He will ever be my joy
I can't wait to cross life's threshold
My willing voice His praise employ.

Take me back to Calvary
Let me see your agony
May I behold the risen Lamb
Who in the storm brought instant calm.

And here remember, nor cease to pray
For relatives, brothers, Thy mercy allay
The sin, the mar, now cast it far
Reclaim their soul, and make it whole.

Beyond the tree, I worship Thee
Seated high above the sky
Lamb of God, Prince of peace
My gratitude shall never cease.

Before the Throne
I come to You alone
Seeking for rest
And to be blessed.

Mindful of your loving grace
The agony suffered in my place
With gratitude I humbly bow
Rejoice You're crowned with Glory now.

Stride afoot o'er hill and dale
From Giant's Causeway to the Pale;
Go tell the Sons of Erin
Jesus died and rose again.

That He saved to sin no more
Let your praises ring galore
For He has come
To bring His children home.

How He died to set men free
And that's all, both you, and me;
Oh hail Him, Christ, Redeemer, King
He is Lord of everything.

To think that You would die for me
At Calvary, what shame for Thee
I owe a debt I cannot pay
My only course is Thee to obey.

There's water here, baptise me clear
This step to take, from past to break;
Rejoice my Saviour lifted high
My soul to save, He choose to die.

And Father love, in Heaven above
Spared not His Son for everyone
What joy to see, travail to glee
The way is clear, and Heaven near.

Redeem the time, don't dwell on crime
The message share, take every care
The bliss to bring, spare not to sing
This bread to break, and of it partake.

Journey's end I see the Light
The Christ of Calvary within sight
Away romance, haste Heaven's chance
My saviour, Master, a time to dance.

What think of me
A sinner saved by grace
I long to see
The salvation of my Race
For Christ has died
To bring His children Home
And me betide
Will seek while Holy Spirit roam.

I, too, will look to Thee
Great Paraclete I cannot see
Yet me inspire
Ablaze with sacred fire
To see Thy Kingdom come
Let us ever beat the drum
Alert our countrymen;
Repent, and be Born Again.

I have this Remembrance to keep
Of Kingly death, beyond all to meet
Jesus slain, volunteer of infinite worth.
Nor can ever repay of earthly birth.

Beyond the skies, I realize, my endless debt
And He no sorrow, no travail dost regret
For He has come to bring His children home
From His Kingdom, alas to Christendom.

Oh Saviour of the world mankind
Forever we've been on your mind
Not least our sins to recompense
Without such love our peril tense.

O may we come to testify
Of grace that took our place to die
Fathomless the love of God
That He the sinners' road would trod.

Merit I nothing from His hand
Simply this do understand
He paid the price, what sacrifice
And I go free, since He died for me.

All glory to the Father be
And Christ who hung upon the tree
Shed I my thanks with all the throng
Bought by Him, to Him belong.

Mercy there tell all the world
Inform them of God's Grace unfurled.
Precious is the Lamb of God
Go to Him before you reach the sod.

Printed in the United States
by Baker & Taylor Publisher Services